£3.00

PASTA & PIZZA
FOR BEGINNERS

Fiona Watt

Designed by Mary Cartwright
Illustrated by Kim Lane
Photography by Howard Allman

Recipes by Julia Kirby-Jones
Food preparation by Ricky Turner and Lizzie Harris
Cover illustration by Christyan Fox

Contents

Before you begin   2
Cooking pasta   4
Pasta recipes   6 -29
Making a pizza base   30
Pizza recipes   32- 47
Index   48

Before you begin

Before you cook any of the recipes in this book, read through the tips on these two pages. They will help you to cook successfully.

Ingredients

At the beginning of each recipe you'll find a list of ingredients which you will need. Make sure that you have them all before you start to cook.

Measuring ingredients

The ingredients' lists show both grammes and ounces for measuring. Follow the recipe using one or the other, but don't mix them up.

Cooking times

All the recipes tell you how long to cook the food, so follow these closely. If you have a fan oven look at its instruction book. Either, shorten the cooking time or turn down the temperature by the amount it says.

Pizza bases

You can find out how to make two different kinds of pizza bases in this book. If you don't have time to make a base, many supermarkets sell ready-made bases. If you use one, just make the pizza topping from the recipe. You can also buy mixes for pizza bases.

Chopping onions

1. Put the onion onto a chopping board and use a vegetable knife to chop off the top and the roots. Take care as you cut.

2. Slice through the papery outside skin. Use a fingernail to lift the skin at the slice then peel the rest of the skin away.

3. Cut the onion in half. Lay the flat side on your chopping board and holding the onion firmly, slice it as finely as you can.

Garlic

A garlic bulb

A clove of garlic

You may need to use a knife to split the skin.

If your recipe uses garlic, it will tell you how many cloves you will need. A clove is one part of a whole bulb of garlic.

1. Squeeze and twist the garlic bulb so that the the outer skin breaks. Pull a clove of garlic off the bottom of the stem.

2. Cut a small piece off the top and bottom of the clove, then peel off the skin. The clove is now ready to use.

Pasta

You can use fresh or dried pasta for all the recipes in this book. You need a different amount depending on the type you use. See the ingredients' lists.

Mushrooms

Don't wash mushrooms before you use them but wipe them clean with a damp paper towel. Cut off the end of the stalk.

Mozzarella cheese

The recipes in this book use two types of Mozzarella cheese. If the recipe says to use 'Mozzarella cheese', use the kind you buy in a plastic bag, surrounded by liquid. The other kind is written as 'grated Mozzarella'. You can buy this ready-grated or as a large solid block.

Mozzarella cheese is soft and you can't grate it. Slit the bag you buy it in and pour away the liquid, before you slice it.

Grated Mozzarella is firmer than the other kind. Some supermarkets sell it as 'pizza cheese'.

Types of pasta

Each of the pasta recipes in this book suggests a type of pasta for you to cook, but in most cases you can use any shape you like. Many supermarkets sell lots of different kinds of fresh and dried pasta. If you see the words 'rigate' on a packet of pasta, it just means that it has a ridged surface.

Tortellini (little twists). These are often stuffed with spinach, cheese or meat.

Tagliarini. Tagliatelle is like this but is thicker.

Macaroni (tubes)

Ravioli. These are usually filled with meat but sometimes with vegetables, fish or cheese.

Fusilli (spirals)

Conchigliette (little shells)

Conchiglie giganti

Conchiglie (shells)

Penne (quills)

Egg noodles

Cooking pasta

The amount of time you need to cook pasta depends on its type and shape. Fresh pasta and long thin shapes cook more quickly than dried pasta or chunky shapes. Try not to overcook your pasta. It should be firm, not soggy.

Make the pan three-quarters full.

Oil stops the pasta from sticking.

1. Fill a very large saucepan with water. Turn on the heat and bring the water to boil. While the water is heating, weigh your pasta on some kitchen scales.

2. When the water is boiling and the surface looks as if it is 'rolling', not just bubbling, add a teaspoon of salt and a tablespoon of cooking oil.

3. Add the pasta to the pan and stir it to separate it. When you add the pasta the water will stop boiling. Turn up the heat and bring it to boiling again.

Turn down the heat if the water looks as if it will boil over.

4. Start to time your cooking, following the instructions on the packet of pasta, from when the water boils with the pasta in it.

5. When the pasta has cooked for the correct time, hold a colander over a sink and pour the pasta into it. You may need help to hold the pan.

6. If you need to leave your pasta in a colander, put a little butter on it. Toss the pasta so that it is coated. Put a plate on top to keep it warm.

Cooking spaghetti

When you cook dried spaghetti, hold one end and gently press it into the water as it softens. Use a spoon to press the ends under the water.

Vermicelli (little worms)

Red pasta has tomato in it and green pasta is made with spinach.

Spaghetti

Farfalle (butterflies)

Spaghetti alla carbonara

Serves 4

375g (12oz) dried spaghetti,
   or 450g (15oz) fresh spaghetti

For the sauce: 200g (8oz) streaky bacon or ham
1 large onion
2 cloves of garlic
1 tablespoon of cooking oil
3 eggs
3 tablespoons of single cream
ground black pepper
40g (1½ oz) grated Parmesan cheese
40g (1½ oz) butter
1 level tablespoon of chopped parsley

Add the spaghetti when the water is boiling.

Stir the onion and garlic as they are cooking.

1. Peel and chop the onion. Snip the rind off the bacon and cut the rashers in strips 1cm (½ in) wide. Peel and crush the garlic (see right).

2. Read the instructions on the packet of spaghetti to find out how long it will take to cook. Weigh it and start to cook it.

3. Heat the oil gently in a frying pan. Add the onion and garlic, and cook them for about five minutes until they are soft.

Stir the mixture as it is cooking.

Turn off the heat when you drain the spaghetti.

4. Add the bacon or ham. If you are using bacon, cook it until it is brown and crispy. If you are using ham, cook it until it is hot.

5. Use a fork to beat the eggs, cream, a pinch of black pepper and most of the cheese to make a creamy mixture.

6. When the spaghetti is cooked, drain it then put it back into the pan. Add the butter and toss the spaghetti until it is coated.

The heat from the spaghetti cooks the egg.

7. Add the bacon, onion and garlic then stir in the cheesy mixture. Use a fork to toss the spaghetti quickly, until it is coated.

8. Put the spaghetti onto four plates or bowls. Sprinkle on the parsley and the rest of the cheese. Serve immediately.

Crushing garlic

Put your hand on the spoon and press hard several times.

If you don't have a garlic crusher, put a clove of garlic on a chopping board. Put the back of a spoon onto it and press down.

Garlic mushroom pasta

Serves 4

400g (14oz) dried fusilli,
  or 500g (1 lb) fresh fusilli

For the sauce: 75g (3oz) butter
450g (1 lb) mushrooms
1 clove of garlic
salt and ground black pepper
200g (7oz) crème fraîche

1. Fill a pan with water and bring it to the boil. Weigh your pasta and add it to the pan. Leave it cooking.

2. Slice the mushrooms thinly. Peel and crush the garlic. Gently melt the butter in a pan. Add the mushrooms and garlic.

3. Add a pinch of salt and pepper to the pan and cook the mixture for about five minutes, stirring occasionally.

Serve your pasta on plates or in large, flat bowls.

4. Drain the pasta and add it to the mushrooms. Add the crème fraîche and stir it until it melts. Serve immediately.

This three-coloured pasta is called 'tricolori fusilli'.

Spicy sausage pasta

Serves 4

400g (14oz) dried conchiglie,
  or 500g (1 lb) fresh conchiglie

For the sauce: 2 tablespoons of olive oil
1 onion
1 clove of garlic
400g (14oz) tin of chopped tomatoes
4 chorizo sausages
1 tablespoon of chopped parsley

1. Peel the onion and slice it finely. Peel and crush the clove of garlic. Put the oil in a large pan and heat it gently.

The sauce will reduce in amount.

2. Add the onion and garlic. Cook them for five minutes or until the onion is soft. Stir the mixture as it is cooking.

3. Add the tomatoes to the pan and bring it to boil. Turn the heat down and let the sauce bubble gently for 20 minutes.

Chorizo sausages are very spicy. Use kabanos sausages or salami if you don't like spicy food.

4. While the sauce is cooking, put a pan of water on to boil. Cook the pasta following the instructions on its packet.

5. Cut the ends off the sausages. Peel the papery skin off the sausages. Slice each sausage and add the slices to the sauce.

6. Drain the pasta and divide it between four bowls or plates. Spoon the sauce on top and sprinkle with parsley.

Macaroni cheese

Serves 4

175g (6oz) dried macaroni,
   or 200g (7oz) fresh macaroni

For the cheese sauce:
50g (2oz) margarine or butter
50g (2oz) plain flour
600ml (1 pint) milk
1 teaspoon of mustard paste
175g (6oz) Cheddar cheese, grated
salt and pepper

For the topping:
25g (1oz) Cheddar cheese, grated

Heat your oven to 180°C, 350°F, Gas mark 4.

Put the macaroni back into the pan after you have drained it.

Use a wooden spoon to stir.

1. Turn on your oven. Weigh the macaroni. Read the instructions on its packet and cook it for the time it says. Drain it.

2. To make the sauce, melt the margarine or butter in a pan over a low heat. Stir in the flour and cook it for one minute.

3. Take your pan off the heat and add a little milk. Stir it really well. Carry on stirring in the rest of the milk, a little at a time.

Add a pinch of salt and pepper too.

4. Return your pan to the heat and start to bring it to boil, stirring all the time. The sauce will stick if you don't stir it.

5. The sauce will begin to thicken. Let the sauce bubble for a minute then turn off the heat. Stir in the mustard and cheese.

6. Pour the sauce over the cooked macaroni. Stir it well so that the sauce coats all of the pieces of macaroni.

Adding cheese

7. Dip a paper towel into some margarine and rub it inside an ovenproof dish to grease it. Pour in the cheesy macaroni.

8. Sprinkle grated cheese on top. Put the dish into the oven for about 25 minutes, until the top is golden brown.

Add the cheese to a sauce after you have turned off the heat and the sauce coats the back of your spoon when you lift it.

Penne with Bolognese sauce

Serves 4

400g (14oz) dried penne,
   or 500g (1 lb) fresh penne

For the sauce: 2 tablespoons of olive oil
2 rashers of streaky bacon
1 onion
1 carrot
1 stick of celery
1 clove of garlic
250g (8oz) lean minced beef or lamb
225g (8oz) tin of chopped tomatoes
2 tablespoons of tomato purée
1 beef or vegetable stock cube
1 teaspoon of dried basil
freshly ground black pepper

To serve: grated Parmesan cheese

1. Peel or scrape the carrot then grate it. Crush the garlic and chop the bacon, onion and celery finely. Heat the oil in a saucepan over a medium heat.

2. Add the bacon to the pan and cook for three or four minutes. Stir it occasionally. Add all the vegetables and cook them until they are soft.

3. Add the minced beef or lamb to the pan. Break up the meat with a spoon and cook it for six to eight minutes, or until the meat is brown all over.

4. Boil a kettle of water. Crumble the stock cube into a measuring jug and pour in 125ml (4fl oz) of water. Stir it well then add it to the meat.

5. Pour in the tomatoes. Stir in the purée and basil. Put a lid on and let the sauce bubble gently for 30-40 minutes. Remove the lid halfway through.

6. As the sauce is cooking, stir it occasionally to stop it from sticking. It will become thicker and the amount of liquid will reduce.

7. About 15 minutes before the sauce is ready, boil a pan of water. Add the pasta and cook for the time it says on its packet. Drain it and serve immediately.

Spoon the sauce over the hot penne and sprinkle with Parmesan cheese.

Making stock

1. Boil a kettle. Either cut up or crumble a stock cube and put it into a measuring jug.

2. Pour in the amount of water you need for your recipe. Stir it well until the stock cube dissolves.

Pasta with green vegetables

Serves 4

375g (12oz) dried tagliarini
  or 400g (14oz) fresh tagliarini
25g (1oz) butter
4 spring onions
225g (8oz) broccoli
125g (4oz) fine green beans
125g (4oz) mangetout
1 courgette
125g (4oz) soft cheese with
  garlic and herbs

This green and yellow tagliarini is known as 'paglia e fieno' (straw and hay).

Cut the courgette in half across the middle, not lengthways.

1. Chop the top and bottom off the spring onions. Pull off the outer layer. Cut them into pieces, 3cm (1in) long.

2. Use a knife to cut the curly ends off the broccoli stalks. Trim the ends off the green beans and cut them in half.

3. Trim the ends off the mangetout. Chop them in half. Cut the ends off the courgette and cut it in half. Slice it into thin strips.

Cook on a low heat.

4. Fill a pan with water and boil it. Add the broccoli and beans and cook them for three minutes. Drain them.

5. Boil a pan of water for the pasta. Melt the butter in a frying pan. Add the onion, broccoli and beans. Cook them for five minutes.

6. Add the rest of the vegetables. Cook them for a further three minutes, stirring them occasionally.

Trimming vegetables

7. Cook the pasta for three minutes then drain it. Put it back into the pan and add the vegetables. Mix them well.

8. Add the cheese. Break it up with a spoon. Cook over a low heat until the cheese melts. Serve it immediately.

It's easier to use scissors rather than a knife to trim vegetables like beans or mangetout.

Ravioli with tomato sauce

Serves 4

400g (14oz) fresh, or 400g (14oz) dried ravioli
1 tablespoon of olive oil
1 onion
1 clove of garlic
400g (14oz) tin of chopped tomatoes
salt and black pepper
8 basil leaves
125g (4oz) Mozzarella cheese

1. Peel the onion and chop it finely. Peel and crush the garlic. Heat the oil in a saucepan and add the onion and garlic.

2. When the onion and garlic are soft, add some salt and pepper and the tomatoes. Let it bubble gently for 15 minutes.

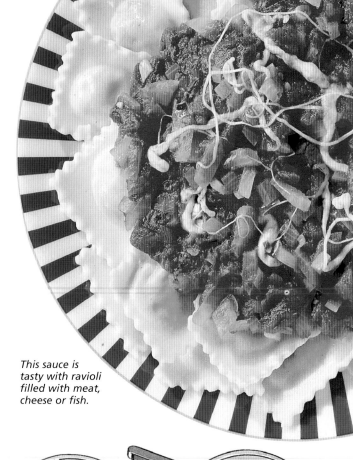

This sauce is tasty with ravioli filled with meat, cheese or fish.

3. While the sauce is cooking, cut the cheese and basil into thin strips. Boil a pan of water for the ravioli.

4. When the water for the pasta is boiling, add the ravioli and cook it, following the instructions on its packet.

5. Just before the pasta is ready, add the cheese and basil to the sauce. Let the cheese melt a little then serve immediately.

Cheesy tortellini

Serves 4

400g (14oz) fresh tortellini
50g (2oz) butter
200ml (7oz) double cream
150ml (½ pint) milk
175g (6oz) Cheddar or Gruyère cheese
1 heaped tablespoon of chopped parsley

Stir it as it cooks.

1. Grate the cheese. Boil a pan of water. Add the tortellini and cook them following the instructions on their packet.

2. Put the butter, cream, milk and cheese into a pan and heat them gently for about five minutes, until the cheese melts.

3. Let the cheese sauce bubble gently for five minutes, stirring it from time to time. Add the chopped parsley.

4. Drain the pasta well and pour it into the cheese sauce. Stir it so that the pasta is coated then eat it immediately.

Spinach and ricotta pasta shells

Serves 4

16 conchiglie giganti (giant pasta shells)

For the filling: 1 onion
1 tablespoon of olive oil
1 clove of garlic
225g (8oz) fresh spinach
225g (8oz) ricotta cheese

For the tomato sauce: 1 onion
1 tablespoon of oil
1 clove of garlic
1 level tablespoon of tomato purée
2 level teaspoons of sugar
400g (14oz) tin of chopped tomatoes
1 tablespoon of fresh chopped basil
salt and black pepper

To serve: grated Parmesan cheese

You can use 175g (6oz) of frozen spinach instead of fresh. Thaw it and drain it well. You don't need to add any water when you heat it at step 4.

1. Fill a large pan with water and bring it to boil. Add the pasta shells and cook them according to their packet.

2. While the pasta is cooking, start to make the filling. Peel the onion and chop it very finely. Peel and crush the garlic.

3. Heat the oil and cook the onion and garlic until they are soft, but don't let them go brown. Spoon them into a mixing bowl.

Stir it as it cooks.

4. Wash the spinach well. Put it into a large pan and cook it over a medium heat for about two minutes.

5. Spoon the spinach into a colander. Press it with the back of a large spoon to squeeze out as much liquid as you can.

6. Put the spinach onto a chopping board and cut it up into small pieces. Use a fork to hold it as it will still be hot.

Toss the pasta in a little butter.

Make the sauce in a big, shallow pan.

7. When the shells are cooked, drain them in a colander and leave them to cool a little. Carry on making the filling.

8. Put the spinach into the bowl along with the ricotta. Add a pinch of salt and pepper and mix everything together.

9. Make the tomato sauce following steps 2 to 5 on page 33. While the sauce is bubbling, begin to fill the pasta shells.

10. Hold the shell in one hand and use a teaspoon to fill each shell with some of the spinach and ricotta mixture.

11. When all the shells are filled, lay them, open-side up into the sauce. Heat them for 10-15 minutes with a lid on top.

12. Spoon four shells and some sauce onto each plate. Sprinkle them with Parmesan cheese and eat them immediately.

Chicken and bacon pasta

Serves 4

400g (14oz) dried tagliatelle,
   or 500g (1 lb) fresh tagliatelle

50g (2oz) margarine or butter
450g (14oz) chicken, without
   any bones
4 rashers of bacon
100g (4oz) mushrooms
4 spring onions
1 teaspoon of chopped parsley
2 level tablespoons of flour
250ml (½ pint) milk
4 heaped tablespoons of crème fraîche
salt and ground black pepper

*Use kitchen
scissors to
cut the bacon.*

*Cook over a
low heat.*

1. Cut the roots off each spring onion. Trim the top and peel off the outer layer. Cut them into 2cm (1in) pieces.

2. Slice the mushrooms finely. Snip any rind off the bacon then cut the rashers into pieces. Put a pan of water on to boil.

3. Chop the chicken into small chunks. Melt the margarine or butter in another saucepan and stir in the chopped chicken.

4. Cook the chicken for five minutes until it loses its pinkness. Cut one piece in half to check that it's cooked right through.

5. Add the bacon to the chicken and cook for three minutes more. Then add the mushrooms and onions to the pan.

6. Cook the mixture for two minutes then stir in the flour. Cook it for a minute then take the pan off the heat.

The sauce will take about a minute to thicken.

7. Gradually add the milk, stirring it all the time. Put the pan back on the heat and let it bubble gently until the sauce thickens.

8. Add the crème fraîche and parsley. Put in a pinch of salt and pepper. Turn the heat as low as it will go while you cook the pasta.

9. Cook the pasta, following the time on its packet. Drain it and put it back into its pan. Stir in the sauce. Eat it immediately.

Meatballs in tomato sauce

Makes 16 meatballs, serves 4

250g (8oz) dried, or 350g (12oz)
fresh egg noodles

For the meatballs:
500g (1lb) minced lean beef or lamb
2 level teaspoons of dried herbs
1 egg
1 tablespoon of flour
cooking oil, preferably olive oil

For the tomato sauce:
1 onion
1 clove of garlic
400g (14oz) tin of chopped tomatoes
1 tablespoon of fresh chopped basil
1 tablespoon of tomato purée
salt and ground black pepper

Use a large mixing bowl.

1. Put the meat into a bowl and break it up with a fork. Crack the egg into a cup then add it, along with the mixed herbs and flour.

2. Wash your hands. Pick up some of the mixture and shape it into a ball, about the size of a table tennis ball. Make 15 more.

3. Heat three tablespoons of oil in a frying pan and add eight meatballs. Turn them often, until they are brown all over.

Always keep raw meat and cooked meat apart.

Stir the onion and garlic as they cook.

4. Put a paper towel onto a plate and lift the browned meatballs onto it. Brown the other eight meatballs and put them on the plate.

5. Chop the onion and peel and crush the garlic. Heat a tablespoon of oil in a saucepan and fry them until they are soft.

6. Add the tomatoes, basil, purée and salt and pepper. Let it boil, then turn down the heat and bubble it gently for ten minutes.

You may have to look in the Oriental food section in your supermarket to find egg noodles. You could use spaghetti or vermicelli instead.

The oil prevents the noodles from sticking together.

Cook the noodles when the meatballs are ready.

7. Add the meatballs. Put a lid onto the pan and leave the sauce to bubble gently for 20 minutes, stirring occasionally.

8. While the meatballs are cooking, half-fill a pan with water and bring it to the boil. Add a tablespoon of oil to the water.

9. Add the noodles, let the water boil again, then simmer for the time it says on their packet. Drain and serve with the meatballs.

Minestrone soup

Serves 4

4 rashers of bacon or pancetta
2 sticks of celery
2 medium-sized potatoes
2 carrots
1 onion
1 leek
1 clove of garlic
1 tablespoon of cooking oil, preferably olive oil
1 tablespoon of tomato purée
2 stock cubes
1 litre (2 pints) of water
1 teaspoon of mixed dried herbs
a quarter of a small dark green cabbage
50g (2oz) small dried pasta shapes
50g (2oz) frozen peas
salt and ground black pepper

To serve: 50g (2oz) grated Parmesan cheese

Instead of using pasta shapes, you could use spaghetti broken into small pieces.

1. Use a clean pair of kitchen scissors to remove the rind from the bacon. Snip the rashers into strips about 2cm (¾ in) wide.

2. Peel the potatoes and cut them in half. Cut each piece into 1cm (½ in) slices. Then cut the slices into cubes.

3. Wash the celery and the leek, and peel the carrots. Cut them all into thin slices. Peel the garlic. Peel the onion and slice it.

4. Heat the oil in a saucepan. Add the bacon. Cook it for a few minutes until it is brown then crush the garlic into the pan.

5. Add all the vegetables you have chopped and stir them well. Let them cook for five minutes, stirring them often.

6. Crumble the stock cube into a measuring jug and pour in 500ml (1 pint) of boiling water. Add the tomato purée and stir well.

Cut out the stalk before you slice it.

7. Pour the stock mixture into the pan, Add another 500ml (1 pint) of water, along with the herbs and a pinch of salt and pepper.

8. Turn up the heat so that the mixture boils. Put a lid on the pan and let the sauce bubble gently for about 20 minutes.

9. Meanwhile, remove the outer leaves from the quarter of cabbage and wash it. Cut it into very thin slices.

10. Add the cabbage and pasta to the pan and let it boil. Turn the heat down and cover it. Cook it for ten more minutes.

11. Add the peas to the pan and stir them in well. Let the soup cook for another two minutes until the peas have heated up.

12. Use a ladle to spoon the soup into four bowls. Sprinkle a little Parmesan cheese on top of the soup and eat it immediately.

Stir fry with vermicelli

Serves 4

175g (6oz) dried vermicelli,
   or 225g (8oz) fresh vermicelli
3 tablespoons of soy sauce
1 tablespoon of lemon juice
1 tablespoon of clear honey
3cm (1in) piece of fresh ginger
285g (10oz) boneless chicken breast
2 carrots
1 red pepper
1 clove of garlic
100g (4oz) mangetout
100g (4oz) baby sweetcorn
100g (4oz) mushrooms
4 spring onions
1 tablespoon of sunflower oil
a vegetable stock cube

1. Cut the light brown skin off the piece of ginger. Cut the ginger into thin slices, then cut the slices into very thin strips.

2. Put the soy sauce, lemon juice and honey in a bowl. Add the pieces of ginger and stir them well. This is your marinade.

3. Cut the chicken into strips about 2cm (¾ in) wide. Add it to the marinade and stir well. Leave it for half an hour.

See the tip on page 41.

4. While the chicken is marinading, make 150ml (½ pint) of stock (see page 13). Peel the carrots and cut them into thin 'sticks'.

5. Cut the ends off the pepper. Chop it in half and cut out the seeds. Slice the pepper into thin strips. Peel and crush the garlic.

6. Cut the stalks off the mangetout and slice the top off the sweetcorn. Cut them all in quarters. Slice the mushrooms.

Stir it all the time.

7. Trim the ends off the spring onions, then cut them into pieces about 3cm (1in) long. Put a pan of water on to boil.

8. Heat the oil in a frying pan. When the oil is hot, add the garlic. Spoon in the chicken, leaving your marinade in the bowl.

9. Cook the chicken for five minutes. When all the pinkness has gone, add all the vegetables to the pan.

10. Stir the vegetables for three minutes. Pour in the stock and marinade and let it boil. Cook for two more minutes.

11. Add the vermicelli to the pan of boiling water. Boil it for three minutes, stirring occasionally then drain it well.

12. Add the vermicelli to the vegetables and stir it in. Leave the mixture for a minute then eat it immediately.

Tuna and tomato pasta salad

Serves 4

300g (10oz) dried farfalle,
or 375g (12oz) fresh farfalle
400g (14oz) tin of tuna
10 cherry tomatoes
175g (6oz) thin green beans

For the dressing:
4 tablespoons of mayonnaise
4 tablespoons of milk
salt and black pepper
4 fresh chives

Toss the pasta with some butter.

1. Fill a large saucepan with water and bring it to the boil. Weigh the pasta and add it to the pan when it is boiling.

2. Cook the pasta following the instructions on its packet. Pour the pasta into a colander to drain it. Leave it to cool.

3. Use kitchen scissors to snip the ends off the beans. Cut the beans in half. Put on a pan of water to boil.

4. When the water is boiling, add the beans and cook them for five minutes. Drain them and rinse them with cold water.

5. Open the tin of tuna. Tip it into a sieve to drain away the liquid. Put it on a saucer and use a fork to break it up a little.

6. Put the pasta, beans, and tuna into a large bowl and mix them. Cut the tomatoes in half and add them to the bowl.

Instead of making a dressing, you could toss your salad in a ready-made one.

7. Put the mayonnaise and milk into a bowl and add a pinch of salt and pepper. Use a fork to mix them together well.

8. Pour the dressing ove the pasta mixture. Use fork to toss the mixtur the dressing so that it covered.

9. Use kitchen sc
snip the chives i
pieces and scatt
over the top. Sp
salad onto plat

Making a pizza base

This traditional pizza dough will make a round pizza 25cm (10in) across, or a rectangular one 35 x 25cm (14 x 10in).

350g (12oz) strong plain flour
1 teaspoon of salt
15g (½oz) fresh yeast, or 1 teaspoon of easy blend yeast
200ml (7fl oz) of warm water
1 tablespoon of olive oil
margarine for greasing

a baking sheet or tray, about 35 x 25cm (14 x 10in)

Cook your pizza on a large baking sheet or on a baking tray like this.

ˈ should take about 15 ˈnutes to go frothy.

are using fresh
x it with a little
ˈm water. Leave
ˈ place until it

If you are using easy blend yeast, open the packet, but don't add any warm water to it now. Add all the water at step 2.

2. Use a sieve to sift the flour and salt. Add the oil, yeast mixture and the rest of the warm water. Stir them well.

r
a
ˈe in
ˈis

ˈssors to
ˈto small
ˈr them
ˈoon the
ˈs or bowls.

29

4. Sprinkle flour onto a clean, dry work surface ˈnd knead the dough well ˈtil it is smooth and ˈtchy (see right).

5. Dip a paper towel into some margarine and rub it inside a large bowl to grease it. Put the dough into the bowl.

Kneading

The dough stretches as you push it.

1. Use the heels of both hands, or your knuckles, to push the dough away.

2. Fold the dough in half and turn it around. Push it away from you again.

3. Fold and turn the dough again. Push it away from you as you did before.

4. Carry on folding, turning and pushing until the dough feels smooth and stretchy.

6. Cover the bowl with plastic foodwrap. Put it in a warm place for about 45 minutes, or until it has risen to twice its size.

7. Turn your oven on to 220°C, 425°F, Gas mark 7. Grease a baking tray or sheet with margarine. Rub it all over.

8. When the dough has risen, knead it again so that you burst all the large air bubbles in it. It won't take very long.

9. Put the dough onto your baking tray. Press it into the shape you want. Pinch up the edges. It's now ready for its topping.

Neapolitan pizza

Serves 6 - makes a rectangular pizza
30 x 25cm (14 x 10in)

One traditional pizza base - see pages 30-31

For the tomato sauce: 1 tablespoon of olive oil
1 onion
1 clove of garlic
1 tablespoon of tomato purée
400g (14oz) tin of chopped tomatoes
2 teaspoons of sugar
1 tablespoon of fresh basil, chopped,
   or 2 teaspoons of dried basil
salt and ground black pepper

For the topping: 250g (8oz) Mozzarella cheese
50g (2oz) tin of anchovy fillets
1 tablespoon of fresh basil, chopped,
   or 2 teaspoons of dried basil
50g (2oz) black olives (without their stones)

Heat your oven to 220°C, 425°F, Gas mark 7

1. Turn on your oven. Follow pages 30-31 to make a pizza base. While the dough is rising, make the tomato sauce.

2. Chop the onion finely and crush the garlic. Put a tablespoon of oil into a medium-sized pan and heat it gently.

3. Add the onion to the pan and stir it on and off for about five minutes until it has softened. Try not to let it go brown.

4. Add the garlic, tomato purée, tomatoes, sugar, basil and a pinch of salt and pepper. Stir it and let the mixture bubble gently.

5. Leave the sauce to cook for 20 minutes or until the sauce becomes thicker and the amount has reduced.

6. When your dough has risen, grease your baking tray with margarine. Place the dough in the middle of the tray.

7. Press the dough out with your fingers to make a rectangle about 30 x 25cm (14 x 10 in). Pinch up the edges to make a rim.

8. Use a spoon to spread the tomato sauce all over the base. Slice the cheese thinly and lay the slices over the sauce.

9. Open the tin of anchovies carefully and drain out the oil. Cut each anchovy in half lengthways.

10. Lay the anchovies in diagonal lines across the pizza. Make lines the other way to make a criss-cross pattern.

11. Sprinkle the basil all over the top then put an olive in the middle of each diamond shape made by the anchovies.

12. Put the pizza into the oven to bake for about 20 minutes, until the base is crisp and golden. Serve the pizza immediately.

Quick Margherita pizza

Makes one 30cm (12in) round pizza.
This recipe uses a scone base, rather than the
traditional base on pages 30-31.

For the scone base: 225g (8oz) self-raising flour
½ a teaspoon of salt
2 tablespoons of cooking oil
150ml (¼ pint) of water

For the topping: 1 tablespoon of cooking oil
2 onions
400g (14oz) tin of plum tomatoes
1 teaspoon of mixed dried herbs
salt and ground black pepper
225g (8oz) Mozzarella cheese

Heat your oven to 200ºC, 400ºF, Gas mark 6

*Make sure that your
work surface is clean
and dry, first.*

1. To make the base, use a
sieve to sift the flour and
salt. Add the oil and water.
Use a round-ended knife to
mix them to make dough.

2. Grease a baking tray
with margarine on a paper
towel. Sprinkle flour onto
your work surface. Knead
the dough (see page 31).

3. Rub a little flour onto a
rolling pin. Gently roll the
dough, turning between
each roll, into a circle
about 30cm (12in) across.

*Pinch
up a rim
around
the edge.*

4. Carefully lift up one
edge of the dough and
slide the rolling pin under
it. Lift the dough onto
your baking tray.

5. To make the topping,
peel the onions and chop
them finely. Gently heat
the oil and cook the
onions until they are soft.

6. While the onions are
cooking, open the tin of
tomatoes and drain them
in a sieve. Chop them into
small pieces.

This pizza is delicious eaten hot or cold.

7. Add the tomatoes and herbs to the onion. Add a pinch of salt and pepper and cook the mixture for ten minutes.

8. Use a spoon to spread the topping over the base. Cut the cheese in thin slices then lay them all over the topping.

9. Bake your pizza in the oven for 25-30 minutes. The base will rise as it cooks and the cheese will go golden.

Mini pizzas

Makes 4 pizzas 15cm (6in) across

One traditional pizza base - see pages 30-31

For the toppings: 2 slices of cooked ham
1 pineapple ring
1 tomato
2 large basil leaves
25g (1oz) sliced pepperoni
2 small mushrooms
25g (1oz) peeled prawns
a small tin of sweetcorn
125g (4oz) grated Mozzarella cheese

Heat your oven to 220°C, 425°F, Gas mark 7

Cut the dough in half, then in half again.

1. Follow the steps on pages 30-31 to make the dough for the bases. When the dough has risen turn on your oven.

2. Put the dough on a floury work surface. Cut it into four and roll each piece into a 15cm (6in) circle. Pinch up the edges.

3. Grease a baking sheet and put the dough circles onto it. Put a tablespoon of milk in a cup and brush each circle with the milk.

4. Cut the ham into small squares. Put these onto one of the bases. Chop up the pineapple ring and lay the pieces on the ham.

5. Slice the tomato finely. Lay them on another base. Cut the basil into small strips and sprinkle them on top.

Try different combinations of ingredients, such as tomato, prawn and mushroom.

6. Lay the slices of pepperoni on the third base. Slice the mushrooms finely and spread them on top of the pepperoni.

7. Open the tin of sweetcorn and drain it. Spread a tablespoon of sweetcorn over the base. Put the prawns on top.

8. Sprinkle each of the pizzas with cheese. Bake them for 15-20 minutes until the bases and cheese are golden brown.

Chicago pizza pie

Makes one 23cm (9in) deep pan pizza

For the dough: 50g (2oz) strong white flour
125g (4oz) plain flour
1 teaspoon of salt
15g (½ oz) fresh yeast,
   or 1 teaspoon of easy blend yeast
200ml (7fl oz) warm water
  1 tablespoon of oil

For the tomato sauce: half a tablespoon of olive oil
  half an onion, finely chopped
  1 clove of garlic
  200g (7oz) tin of chopped tomatoes
  1 teaspoon of chopped basil
  salt and ground pepper

For the topping: 1 green pepper
  50g (2oz) button mushrooms
  50g (2oz) sliced pepperoni
  175g (6oz) grated Mozzarella cheese

a 23/25cm (9/10in) deep pizza tin or sandwich tin

Heat your oven to 220°C, 425°F, Gas mark 7

1. Follow steps 1-8 on pages 30-31 to make the dough. At step 2, sift both types of flour into the bowl.

2. Put a little oil onto a paper towel and rub over the base and inside of the tin so that they are covered with oil.

3. Sprinkle a little flour onto your work surface and on your rolling pin. Roll the dough into a circle about the size of your tin.

4. Place the dough in the middle of the tin and press it out to the edges with your knuckles. Make it as even as you can.

5. Cover the tin with plastic foodwrap and leave it in a warm place for 20 minutes. It will rise a little bit more.

6. Turn on your oven. While the dough is rising, follow steps 2 to 5 on page 33 to make the tomato sauce.

*See the
tip on page
41 for cutting peppers.*

7. Cut the ends off the pepper. Chop it in half and cut out the seeds. Cut it into cubes. Slice the mushrooms thinly.

8. Spread the sauce over the dough. Lay the pepperoni, then the mushrooms and finally the green pepper, on top.

9. Sprinkle it with grated cheese and bake it for about 20 minutes until the dough is golden and has risen.

Prawn pizza

Makes one 25cm (10in) round pizza

One traditional pizza base - see pages 30-31

For the tomato sauce: 1 tablespoon of olive oil
1 onion
1 clove of garlic
1 level tablespoon of tomato purée
450g (14oz) tin of chopped tomatoes
2 teaspoons sugar
1 tablespoon of chopped fresh basil
salt and freshly ground pepper

For the topping: ½ a red pepper
½ a yellow or green pepper
150g (6oz) peeled prawns, thawed, if
    they have been frozen
1 level tablespoon of chopped parsley
1 tablespoon of olive oil

Heat your oven to 220°C, 425°F,
Gas mark 7

Sprinkle flour on your work surface.

Pinch up a rim around the edge.

1. Follow pages 30-31 to make a pizza base. While the dough is rising, make a tomato sauce following steps 2 to 5 on page 33.

2. When your dough has risen and you have kneaded it again, roll the dough into a 25cm (10in) circle. Turn on your oven.

3. Dip a paper towel in margarine and rub it over a baking sheet to grease it. Lay the dough in the middle of the sheet.

4. Cut the seedy part out of the peppers. Slice them lengthways into strips. Try to cut them as finely as you can (see right).

5. Spread the tomato sauce over the base. Scatter the strips of pepper all over it. Sprinkle it with parsley.

6. If your prawns were frozen, put them into a sieve to drain away any liquid, then scatter them over the top.

You can buy lots of different colours of peppers. It doesn't matter which one you choose for this pizza.

7. Sprinkle on some salt and a little black pepper then carefully drizzle the oil from the spoon all over the top.

8. Put your pizza into the oven and bake it for about 20 minutes until the base is crisp and becomes golden brown.

Slicing peppers

When you slice a pepper, cut it in half then cut out the seeds. Slice it from the inside. It's easier than trying to pierce the skin.

Tomato and courgette pizza

Makes one rectangular pizza 30 x 25cm (14 x 10in)

One scone pizza base (see page 34)

For the topping: 1 tablespoon of olive oil
1 onion
2 cloves of garlic
3 beef tomatoes
1 tablespoon of fresh chopped basil
2 tablespoons of pine nuts
1 small courgette
salt and ground black pepper
150g (6oz) grated Mozzarella cheese

Heat your oven to 200°C, 400°F,
Gas mark 6

1. Turn on your oven before you make the dough. Follow steps 1-3 on page 34 to make a scone dough pizza base.

2. Put the dough onto a floured surface and roll and stretch it into a rectangle about 35 x 28cm (14 x 11in).

3. Grease your baking sheet with margarine and carefully lift the dough onto it. Pinch up the edge all the way around.

4. Peel the onion and slice it into thin rings. Crush the garlic. Gently heat the oil and cook the onion and garlic for three minutes.

5. Spread the onion rings and garlic over the dough. Cut the tomatoes in half and slice them as thinly as you can.

6. Lay the tomatoes on the base, overlapping them a little. Scatter the pine nuts and chopped basil over the top.

7. Trim the ends off the courgette. Hold it in one hand and run a potato peeler along to cut really thin slices.

8. Scatter the courgette slices over the pizza. Season it with a little salt and pepper. Sprinkle on the grated cheese.

9. Put the pizza into the oven and bake for 15-20 minutes until the cheese is golden and bubbling. Serve immediately.

Calzones (folded pizzas)

Makes eight calzones

One traditional pizza base (see pages 30-31)

For the filling: 250g (8oz) ricotta cheese
75g (3oz) smoked ham
100g (4oz) Mozzarella cheese
3 large tomatoes
salt and ground black pepper
olive oil

Heat your oven to 220°C, 450°F, Gas mark 7

1. Follow the steps on pages 30-31 to make traditional dough. While it is rising, chop up the ingredients for the filling.

2. Cut the ham into small pieces. Cut the tomatoes and the Mozzarella into small chunks. Turn on your oven.

3. Put both types of cheese, the tomatoes, ham and a pinch of salt and pepper into a bowl. Mix them together well.

Trim the edge to make a circle if you need to.

4. When the dough has risen and you have kneaded it a second time, cut it into eight pieces. Roll the pieces into balls.

5. Sprinkle flour onto a work surface and roll out one of the balls to make a circle about 18cm (7in) across.

6. Put a heaped tablespoon of the mixture onto one half of the circle. Brush a little water around the edge.

6. Fold the dough over the mixture and pinch along the edges to seal the two halves. Make seven more like this.

7. Grease a baking tray with margarine. Lift the calzones onto the tray. Brush them with olive oil and put them in the oven.

8. Bake the calzones for about 20-30 minutes until they have puffed up and have become golden brown.

You can eat the calzones when they are hot or cold.

Patterned edges

Instead of pinching the dough together, you can press a fork around the edge. This leaves a pattern once the calzone is cooked.

Hot apple pizza

Makes one 25cm (10in) round pizza

For the base: 175g (6oz) strong white flour
25g (1oz) butter or margarine
1 teaspoon of easy blend yeast
4 tablespoons of apple juice

For the topping: 2 medium cooking apples
3 tablespoons of apple juice
50g (2oz) raisins
½ a teaspoon of cinnamon
1 tablespoon of sugar
3 eating apples
2 tablespoons of lemon juice
1 heaped tablespoon of brown sugar

Heat your oven to 200°C, 400°F, Gas mark 6

Rub in with your fingers.

1. Sift the flour into a bowl and add the butter or margarine. Rub the butter into the flour until it looks like breadcrumbs.

2. Put the apple juice into a pan and heat it a little to make it warm. Add it, and the yeast to the bowl and stir them well.

3. Continue to stir until you get a soft dough which doesn't stick to the sides of the bowl. Then squeeze it to make a ball.

4. Sprinkle flour onto a clean, dry work surface. Knead the dough until it is smooth and stretchy (see page 31).

Lay the circle of dough onto your baking sheet.

5. Grease a baking sheet with margarine. Rub some flour onto a rolling pin and roll the dough into a 25cm (10in) circle.

6. Pinch up the edge of the dough to make a rim, then cover it with plastic foodwrap. Put it in a warm place for 30 minutes.

7. Peel the cooking apples and cut them in quarters. Cut out the core and then slice the rest of the apple as finely as you can.

8. Put the sliced apple into a small pan. Add the apple juice and cook them with a lid on for 15 minutes until the apple is very soft.

9. Take the pan off the heat and stir the apple to make a smooth sauce, or purée. Add the raisins, sugar and cinnamon.

Cut out the apple cores.

10. Turn the oven on. Peel the eating apples and quarter them. Slice them finely and sprinkle the slices with lemon juice.

11. Spread the purée over the dough with a spoon. Arrange the slices of apple on top, overlapping them a little.

12. Sprinkle the pizza with the brown sugar. Put it into your oven for about 15 minutes or until the dough is golden.

Index

apple pizza, 46

calzones (folded pizzas), 44
carbonara, spaghetti alla, 6
cheese, macaroni, 10
cheese sauce, 11
cheesy tortellini, 17
Chicago pizza pie, 38
chicken and bacon pasta, 20
chopping onions, 3
cleaning mushrooms, 3
cooking pasta, 5
cooking spaghetti, 5
crushing garlic, 3, 6

dough,
　patterns, 45
　scone, 34
　traditional, 30
dried pasta, 2

folded pizza (calzone), 44
fresh pasta, 2

garlic, 3
grated Mozzarella cheese, 3

hot apple pizza, 46

kneading dough, 31

macaroni cheese, 10
making stock, 13
Margherita pizza, 34
meatballs in tomato sauce, 22
minestrone soup, 24
mini pizzas, 36
Mozzarella cheese, 3
mushroom and garlic sauce, 9
mushrooms, 3

Neapolitan pizza, 32
pasta,
　dried, 2
　fresh, 2
　how to cook, 5

types of, 2, 5
with green vegetables, 14
pasta sauces,
　Bolognese, 12
　carbonara, 6
　cheese, 10
　chicken and bacon, 20
　mushroom and garlic, 9
　spicy sausage, 9
　tomato, 16, 22, 33
penne with Bolognese sauce, 12
pizza bases, 2
　making, 30
　scone, 34
　traditional, 30
pizzas,
　apple, 46
　calzones, (folded pizza), 44
　Chicago, 38
　Margherita, 34
　mini, 36
　Neapolitan, 32
　prawn, 40
　tomato and courgette, 42
prawn pizza, 40

quick Margherita pizza, 34

ricotta and spinach pasta shells, 18
ravioli with tomato sauce, 16

scone pizza base, 34
slicing peppers, 41
soup, minestrone, 24
spaghetti, 5
spaghetti alla carbonara, 6
spinach and ricotta pasta shells, 18
stir fry with vermicelli, 26

tomato and courgette pizza, 42
tomato and tuna pasta salad, 28
tomato sauce, 33
tortellini, cheesy, 17
traditional pizza base, 30
trimming vegetables, 15
tuna and tomato pasta salad, 28

First published in 1997 by Usborne Publishing Ltd., Usborne House, 83-85 Saffron Hill, London, EC1N 8RT, England.
Copyright © 1997 Usborne Publishing Ltd. The name Usborne and the device ♈ are Trademarks of Usborne
Publishing Ltd. All rights reserved. No part of this publication may be reproduced, stored in a retrieval system or
transmitted in any form or by any means, electronic, mechanical, photocopying,
recording or otherwise, without permission of the publisher.
Printed in Dubai.